TO: Re

From: Nich Kenyon

2016-05-09

MIND-SET ADJUSTMENTS

MAKE SUCCESS WITH TECHNOLOGY
YOUR NEW NORMAL

Nick Kenyeres

ISBN: 978-1-4834-1888-9 (sc)
ISBN: 978-1-4834-1887-2 (e)

Library of Congress Control Number: 2014917300

Lulu Publishing Services rev. date: 9/30/2014

Contents

Acknowledgments

I would like to thank my good business friend, Suzanne Mladenovich, president of Marketing and Training Solutions (Mtraining.com), for her continued support and encouragement while writing this book. I am very grateful for the heartfelt discussions and spiritual connection we shared, which made it possible for me to capture the true essence of my inner-most thoughts and feelings as they appear in the pages that follow.

I would also like to thank my wife and spiritual partner, Carol, who encourages me to live by my purpose, which is to help people gain a competitive advantage through the innovative use of technology and best practices.

I am eternally grateful!

Foreword

This book was written to help people deal with one of life's most challenging issues: technology! As Nick Kenyeres points out, it isn't the technology itself that allows fear and uncertainty to creep into our lives, but rather, it's the way we think and respond to it that does.

He goes on to state that it's not that we don't accept change, because we do, it's just that we resist being changed in order to *deal* with such change. This in turn prevents us from being all that we can be.

So, to help us overcome our resistance, Nick created a program (and now book) called Mind-Set Adjustments. This program, currently used in his consulting practice, helps us to break through our constraints in thinking that keep us from making real progress in our lives.

Although the mind-set adjustments are based on some simple truths and sound principles, my heart tells me that they can be applied to help us with many of life's challenges and not just with technology alone.

So, if you believe that you have the power to create a new and better reality for yourself in our world of technological expansion but don't know how to, this could be the book you have been waiting for.

You never know, you may only be one mind-set adjustment away from doing so!

Suzanne Mladenovich,
President of Marketing and Training Solutions (Mtraining.com)

Preface

Over the years, I developed an interest in technology and for helping people gain a competitive advantage through the innovative use of technology and best practices.

My interest in technology started in the early 1960s when my parents gave me a transistor radio as a birthday present. This gift not only sparked my interest in radio but also inspired me to build my own radios from parts I extracted from discarded radio and television sets.

When it came time to enter high school, I chose to enroll in a four-year science technology and trades program to explore different trades. During my time there, I studied auto mechanics, electricity, electronics, machining, and woodworking, but my "inner voice" kept telling me that the field of electronics was where I truly belonged.

After graduating from Stamford Collegiate Vocational Institute (1969), I enrolled in the three-year electronics engineering technology diploma program at Niagara College of Applied Arts and Technology. I guess that this wasn't too much of a surprise knowing my history with radio.

While there (1969–1973), I was introduced to a variety of advanced analog, digital, and computer-based technologies, all of which helped me to secure a meaningful position as an aircraft/radar technician for a military contractor.

For the next two years, I spent my time installing crash locators, calibrating fuel cells, and testing radomes—things used in a variety of military aircraft. Although I loved the work, things came to an abrupt end when the company decided not to renew its military-based contract.

I must admit that I was very disappointed, but because of my upbringing, I knew that things always happened for a reason. And as luck (or fate) would have it, I learned about, applied for, and landed a job in the telecommunications industry.

From 1975–1993, I gained invaluable technical experience and knowledge designing, developing, implementing, and selling advanced data and telecommunication solutions.

Experience that compelled me to develop a technical training program to help non-engineering business professionals feel more comfortable with the technologies they were selling.

When a good friend of mine learned about this, he suggested that I contact Sheridan Institute of Advanced Learning and Technology to see if they would be interested in offering it as a special interest course through continuing education. Needless to say, I acted on his advice and they accepted my proposal.

As the course grew in popularity, five courses were added and the program was expanded into a certificate program. The program's success didn't go unnoticed, however, and people started to ask why I wasn't doing this on a full-time basis.

It was a question that I just couldn't get out of my mind.

But after thinking about it for a several months, I realized that it was just part of a much bigger plan, and that the question was merely the catalyst needed to get me to take some definitive action.

And, without getting into the details, I spent the next three years (1993–1996) developing my sales skills and preparing to start my own training business. And on April 1, 1996, The Technology Coach, Inc. was born.

The goal—*to design, develop, and deliver technical training for non-engineering business professionals so their eyes don't glaze over in front of their customers.*

Things went extremely well until September 11, 2001, when terrorists struck New York City, sending many training companies (including mine) into a downward spiral. Instead of getting down on myself, I decided to use my free time wisely by returning to school to get a degree.

In April 2004, I graduated from Bemidji State University with a four-year bachelor of applied science degree in technology management, and at that point, I shifted my focus from providing classroom-type training to developing screencasts, conducting webinars, and creating online learning modules for corporate accounts.

At the end of 2012, I closed The Technology Coach, Inc., to devote my time to writing this book—a book that contains the seven mind-set adjustments I personally used to overcome my own fears and to combat the uncertainty that held me back for far too many years.

Now that this book has been published, my plan is to continue serving people by helping them to gain a competitive advantage through the innovative use of digital technology and best practices.

CHAPTER 1

Introduction

Some people believe that there are only two certainties in life: death and taxes. But, I truly believe that technology needs to be added to the mix.

Death, Taxes, and Technology

Perhaps it's just me, but after witnessing how people deal with technology, I have to believe that my suggestion has some merit.

So why hasn't anyone amended this long-held statement of belief before? After all, it seems logical, reasonable, and completely indefensible.

However, I must emphasize that it isn't the technology itself that activates the symptoms of stress in people, but rather how they deal with all the changes taking place.

This shouldn't be too much of a surprise knowing how much time we spend learning about new hardware and software, setting up systems, troubleshooting them, creating backups, and making little tweaks (or adjustments) along the way.

And this doesn't even include all of the e-mails, website updates, and social media networking activities, and so forth, that also impinge on our time.

The truth is that activities like these can cause *fear* and *uncertainty* to creep into our lives, which, left unchecked, can cause us to wonder.

Wonder whether we'll get that next big promotion, be able to keep our job, or worse yet, become sidelined by some stress-related disease or illness.

Although we can't put the technology genie back into the proverbial bottle, we do have the power to create a different or new reality for ourselves. But, we must *act* in order to do so.

Perhaps this is what Benjamin Franklin (1705–1790) hinted at when he said, "Never confuse motion with action."

Never Confuse Motion with Action

When I first read his words, I sensed that he was speaking the absolute truth. The truth being that success doesn't come from just going through the motions for appearances sake, but comes from taking definitive *action*.

But, what separates the people who act from those who don't?

I believe that the answer is … commitment.

Commitment

A commitment

- to invest the requisite amount of time to learn something new
- to practice by consciously applying what they have learned

These are the things that successful people do to master their craft or to develop a new skill. These are the same people that we come to love, admire, and even envy as we watch them perform to such a high standard.

Perhaps we pay homage to them because we secretly want to be just like them.

So, take a moment to think about how you might feel stepping into their shoes.

I believe that most people would feel transformed:

- Transformed because their work wouldn't seem like work anymore; it would actually be fun, instead.
- Transformed because their work would seem easier to do and be of greater perceived value.
- Transformed because they wouldn't feel that technology was controlling them, but would feel empowered by it instead.

Perhaps this transformation is the reason why this select group of people strive for mastery and makes it appear so effortless to the rest of us.

But if you asked any of them, they would probably tell you the same thing: It takes time (lots of time), plenty of practice, and a real commitment to be successful.

The truth is that their reality can be your reality. And all you need to do is change the way you think about technology and make some simple adjustments.

Adjustments, I refer to as "mind-set adjustments."

Mind-Set Adjustments

Let me explain: I believe that each person is born with a programmable global positioning system (GPS). While some people learn to program theirs to take them directly to Successville, others inadvertently choose a more roundabout route, which may or may not get them there at all.

The fact is that GPS units can be just as infallible as people. Just ask anyone who forgot to update their maps before setting out on a journey. No doubt you have heard stories about people who turned left onto a one-way street—going in the wrong direction or getting lost because they listened to their GPS instead of their own inner voice.

But one thing is certain: you can only get *there* from *here*, wherever *here* is for you.

Just remember that every step forward has to have a starting point from which it originates. And depending on where your starting point is, *pain* exists. It exists to promote evolution, and its cumulative effect forces us in a new direction, although the mechanism might be more difficult for some than others.

The good news is that for each step you take, you will be advancing. Sure, you might make a wrong turn now and again, but the lessons learned will help you to set your internal GPS to a more optimal route.

But how can you make a commitment if you have a *fear* of the unknown, or feel like you are being eaten alive from the inside out by the *uncertainty* of it all? Although this question haunts many of us, there is hope.

Hope that comes in the form of seven *mind-set adjustments*.

Although I can't guarantee that they will work for you, I do know that they helped me to overcome my own fears and the uncertainty that held me back for far too many years.

So, if you are ready, let's begin this journey, by turning the page.

After all, you aren't alone.

Notes Page

CHAPTER 2

A Call for Action

This book is about survival in an age where new technology weaves its way into the fabric of our lives, forever changing the way we work, live, and play.

For some, technology is viewed as a tool that empowers them to soar to new heights, both personally and professionally; whereas for others, it is seen as an impediment that disrupts their lives and drags them down.

I refer to this as the *great technological divide.*

The Great Technological Divide

On one side of the great technological divide, you have people who are reaping the benefits; on the other, you have people struggling to survive. As a digital lifestyle coach and trainer, I believe that the only thing that separates the people into these two camps is the way they deal with (or handle) change.

Unfortunately, the greatest difficulty associated with change is that most people reject it when it is needed the most. The problem is that by the time they realize that change is needed and that they must shift to a new way of thinking, it is often too late.

And this is where *fear* and *uncertainty* starts to creep into their lives.

- *Fear* causes people to feel overwhelmed, confused, and drained of the energy they need to pursue their goals.

- *Uncertainty* causes people to question whether they should even bother to apply themselves; or they don't see the reason for wanting to subject themselves to the pain of learning something new.

But if you asked these people, they would probably admit that their lives could be so much better; and that they don't need to accept a life of mediocrity or of quiet desperation.

And it's not that these people can't accept change, because they can. It's just that they resist being changed, which allows even more *fear* and *uncertainty* to creep into their lives.

People Fear Being Changed

My guess is that most people don't realize that the things they *fear* the most are based on falsehoods. If they could replace the *false* with the *true*, it would release them from the chains that bind them.

Hopefully, you have heard stories about people who overcame the odds only to become the success they were meant to be.

These are the people who

- Learned how to step out of their comfort zone and to move forward with purpose
- Learned how to overcome their fears and the uncertainty that was holding them back
- Learned how to act and follow through on their ideas

In today's technology-obsessed world, there appears to be too many people that pass up a chance for learning, feel labeled as a failure, or get discouraged when something requires too much time and effort.

Although I can't tell you precisely what each person did to overcome the odds, I am quite certain that *making a commitment* had something to do with it:

- A *commitment* to stand up to the challenge, to learn from their failures, and continue with their efforts
- A *commitment* to invest the requisite amounts of time and effort to learn something new
- A *commitment* to practice by consciously applying what they have learned

But, how can you make such a commitment?

The truth is, you can't unless you are prepared to dig deep (very deep) and find the answer to the "What's in it for me?" (WIIFM) question.

What's In It for Me?

I say this because people need to have a *purpose* for what they do or are about to do before they can make a real *commitment*. For some, this might mean learning to use a spreadsheet program, speaking to a group of people, starting a business, taking a relationship to the next level, learning how to operate a new mobile device, or getting the next promotion.

For me it was all about helping others to gain a competitive advantage through the innovative use of digital technologies and best practices.

The truth is that people with a *purpose* find it easier to make a *commitment* because they have discovered the answer to the WIIFM question. In other words, they found a reason to continue with their efforts.

Find Your Purpose and Everything Changes

So, the trick is to answer the WIIFM-question in a way that will compel you to act, even if it means fooling yourself into changing your beliefs or way of thinking.

But before you answer the all-important WIIFM question, please read each of the chapters in this book and then complete the accompanying exercises.

Although I can't promise that these mind-set adjustments will work for everyone, I do believe that we are all only one adjustment away from making our lives work.

<u>Notes Page</u>

CHAPTER 3

Mind-Set Adjustment Number 1

The first mind-set adjustment is to think of failure as different degrees of success.

Remember, we are all only one adjustment away from making our lives work.

The first thing to do is to look inward to identify the gaps between the *what is* and *what will be* as it relates to your use of technology.

I remember a time when I was enmeshed in my own talent and specialness. But when things went wrong, I lost my focus and my ability putting everything I hoped for into jeopardy. Fortunately, a good friend of mine suggested that I look *inward* to find out why *fear* and *uncertainty* were creeping into my life.

I embraced the challenge and soon realized that I was stuck in the *what is* because I didn't know how to cope with the setbacks that were affecting my well-being. The only way out was to develop new strategies that would enable me to set my internal GPS to a more optimal route.

This caused me to think about my own beliefs and how I always thought that my heroes were born with some advantage. That was until I realized that they were just ordinary people who worked hard to get from the *what is* to the *what will be* in their own area of expertise.

Call it an epiphany or whatever, but I knew then that I would have to work hard and make a real commitment if I was to cross the great technological divide. In fact, all I could think about was one thing; and that was this: Helping others to gain a competitive advantage through the innovative use of digital technologies and best practices.

And, when I looked a little deeper, I started to think about the relationship between practice and improvement and between my mind and my performance.

In fact, this process—of deep thinking—helped me to translate my thoughts into *actions* that fueled my passion: *Passion* that inspires me to spend a disproportionate amount of time practicing and working with computer-based technologies and applying what I was learning.

And interestingly enough, the time spent eventually translated into a new set of skills, and when these skills improved, so did my results. Although this didn't happen overnight, I discovered that the results I was getting provided me with even more enjoyment and passion.

Then suddenly, doors began to open for me, and people started to take notice of my work. It was as if my thoughts were a magnet and I was attracting what my mind was focused on.

It felt as though I was creating my own reality, and I found myself caught in a virtuous cycle which enabled me to produce some extraordinary results.

Results that helped me to understand that success requires action and action requires thought.

Success Requires Action and Action Requires Thought

And on a more fundamental level, this helped me to understand that my own success was the outcome of all of my failures and was the result of all of the little tweaks and adjustments I made along the way.

But to get to this place, I had to make a conscious decision to stop blaming others and to hold myself accountable for my own actions and well-being.

Interesting enough, the real rewards came from the smiles I received helping others and not from the material things or money. This led me to believe that the statement—*the more you give, the more you will receive*—was true.

And through the process of deep thinking, I discovered how to be more confident, happy, and positive by learning to pretend (or act) that I was already this way. And, after practicing being more confident, happy, and positive for many months, I came to the realization that I wasn't pretending anymore.

Just remember that passion leads to inspired action, and our commitment becomes a natural consequence within the process.

And that *success doesn't come from working harder; it comes from working smarter.*

Perhaps this is the kind of thinking that helped Thomas Edison persist as he conducted more than 8,000 experiments to perfect the incandescent light bulb; and something that led me to believe that the trick is to *fool yourself into changing your beliefs or way of thinking until you reach a point where you see incremental improvements and become motivated by that.*

And, when you reach this point, establish some higher-level goals and objectives for yourself to keep propelling yourself forward.

Just remember that your *goals* will tell you where to go, and the data you collect will tell you how you are doing in relation to the *objectives* you have set for yourself.

And don't forget to think of failure as different degrees of success as you follow your heart and learn to listen to your inner voice.

Exercise Number 1: Looking Forward

Part 1: What Is Success?

To start this exercise, think about what success is and what it means to you. And while you are thinking about it, answer the following questions:

1. What will success feel like?
2. What will success look like?
3. How will success change my life?

Knowing "what success is," is important. Otherwise, how will you know when you have arrived?

Part 2: Identifying the Gaps

Once you have defined what success is in your own terms, it's time to look at the things that are keeping you from being the success you are meant to be.

Please note that this step is very important and must *not* be skipped, so spend as much time as you need to answer the following questions.

Just remember that your answers will provide you with some clarity that will help you to get from *what is* to the *what will be* side of the great technological divide.

1. The "What is" question: *What is* your life like now?
2. The "What will be" question: What will your life be like after you master technology?
3. The "Gaps" question: Identify the gaps between the "what is" and the "what will be" in your life. Be completely honest with yourself and spend as much time as you need answering this question.

4. List five to ten goals that you wish to accomplish; then break them down into individual tasks and action steps. Enter the "date to be completed by" beside each one and then start working toward them. This will get you started.

Notes Page

CHAPTER 4

Mind-Set Adjustment Number 2

The second mind-set adjustment is to simplify your life.

Remember, burn the words *"simplicity matters"* deep into you consciousness.

People can be driven to irrational decisions by too much complexity and uncertainty. So, if you are not getting the results you want, try simplifying your life.

This came to me one day as I sat in front of my computer watching a computer manufacture's app counter spinning its way toward 50 billion apps downloaded. Call it an epiphany, or whatever, but I suddenly realized why so many people have problems trying to become master over their computers and mobile devices.

It's the *distractions,* where distractions can be defined as all of the clutter that causes us to become overwhelmed by having too many choices: the clutter that causes us to multitask, even though studies prove that we can't be as effective doing too many things at the same time. As a result, we end up spending more of our precious time working on things that aren't important, causing our productivity to drop.

Although we could blame technology for this, it would be a copout to do so. For example, we could say that a hammer is bad if you strike someone over the head with it; but good if you build a garden shed with it.

The point is that we all have the *power* to make a decision about the role technology will play in our lives, and how much time we spend learning and using it.

My guess is that you wouldn't be reading this book if you didn't want positive change to come into your life. So if technology is causing you to lose site of the finish lines, stopping points, and boundaries, please read on.

Trust me when I say that people of all stripes cry out every day for *simplicity* in their lives.

- *Simplicity* in the activities they pursue
- *Simplicity* in the possessions they own
- *Simplicity* in the technologies they use

But the fact is simplicity is only a part of the answer, because *simplicity can't exist without some complexity*

Simplicity Can't Exist without Some Complexity

But how can we simplify our lives if we keep running away from or avoiding complexity? The answer is that you can't unless you allow some complexity (a *controlled* amount) into your life.

And if you think about it, we all seek rich, satisfying lives. Lives that are only possible when we challenge ourselves and push ourselves beyond our self-imposed limits.

Even our favorite songs, stories, games, and books are rich, satisfying, and complex, which confirms that we need some complexity in our lives even while we crave simplicity.

Perhaps my good business friend Suzanne said it best: "There is *complexity* and *complicated*. *Complexity* is necessary, yet *complicated* introduces confusion much of the time. Therefore, we need to avoid the complicated."

The truth is that all we need to do is find a balance between simplicity and complexity while trying to avoid things that are unnecessarily complicated!

Exercise Number 2: Simplicity Matters

The purpose of this exercise is to simplify your life by eliminating anything that is preventing you from reaching your stated goals.

1. **Use only what you need**: Make a list of all the hardware, software, and mobile devices that you own or sometimes borrow. Beside each item, write a brief statement that identifies what it does, what it is used for, and how often you use it. Be honest! Then eliminate any items that could be considered duplicates, rarely if ever used items, time wasters (such as games), or any items that don't support your cause.

2. **Learn how to use what you have**: Now that you have pared down your list, it's time to take control of your digital life. To do this, learn how to use and make the most of what you have. This can be accomplished by hiring a tutor, taking courses, or through self-study. Remember to start with the items that you need the most and work from there. Just remember to pace yourself.

3. **Make it work the way you want it to work**: As you gain more experience with your technology, think about how you can improve your workflow so that you become more efficient and effective.

4. **Hire a tech advisor**: By the time you reach this stage, you will probably have many questions that are in need of an answer. For example, have you chosen the best technology for your needs? How do you make the software do this or that? What is the best way to simplify my workflow? What should you learn next? A good tech advisor will be able to answer your questions and will be worth every penny spent!

5. **Stay on top of it**: Sometimes the question has to be asked: Why bother? With so many things to do (see 1, 2, 3 and 4 above), it's tempting to take the easy way out and quit. But don't! Just remember that it is possible provided that you don't start to bog yourself down with fabricated *have to* items. I say this because it's very easy to make more work for yourself by trying to do everything alone.

6. **A universal rule**: Although it is difficult for me to come up with a universal rule for you to follow, I can say this: if you've ever asked yourself if something should go, be replaced, or be reworked, just keep asking until it happens. If you're not getting any benefit from it, should you keep wasting your time doing it? Also, if you can fix or replace it for a significant benefit, what are you waiting for?

Notes Page

CHAPTER 5

Mind-Set Adjustment Number 3

The third mind-set adjustment is to adopt a healthy and winning attitude to make it easier to believe in yourself.

Remember, *live from the perspective that all things are possible.*

Success lies in the will and in the belief that whatever you intend is possible. And more important, it is about doing the right thing and not about doing everything right.

You *can* be successful if you *think success.*

The question is how to strengthen the capacity within yourself in order to succeed.

Unfortunately, laziness is one of the main reasons why people fail to reach their full potential. We either procrastinate or give up when we have to deal with all of the day-to-day complexities of our digitized world, such as learning and using computer applications, operating systems, networks, and the like.

Just remember that *you* make yourself feel the way *you* feel. So, start to feel good about yourself, and accept the fact that a little hard work and a *controlled* amount of complexity will empower you.

Think of it as exercise for your mind, a type of exercise that will help you to think and feel better and keep you grounded as you forge ahead.

Learn to be the person who finds the courage to move from the *what is* to the *what will be* side of the great technological divide.

Just remember that it doesn't matter how many disappointments you might have; it is the successful attempts that count the most. These are the things you need to remember and from which you learn.

I must emphasize that empowerment comes from meaning. Those things that have the greatest meaning to us arise from our inner-self and not from the material world around us.

Even if you think that your outer-life is relatively uneventful from one day to the next, you will soon discover that your inner-life is very much alive and rich and full of things that are happening. And as your awareness increases, more insights will begin to occur.

For instance, you will start to perceive the triggers that cause your behavior, and you will become increasingly aware of how you handle yourself and how you could improve. This will cause you to become less *automatic* and more conscious of your choices in each and every situation.

Just remember that success breeds success, and your small successes are stepping stones to greater ones.

Although I have struggled at times, I found solace in believing that my major goals aren't any harder to achieve than my small goals. The key is to find a way to persevere without throwing your hands up in the air. Simply learn from your mistakes and do whatever you can to improve. And although this might sound difficult at first, it can be made so much easier by keeping a journal.

In fact, someone once said that "any life worth living is worth recording."

Any Life Worth Living is Worth Recording

With this truth in mind, let's examine the time-honored method of keeping a journal as a powerful tool for self-improvement.

But before we do, please understand that a journal is not a diary. Although the lines of distinction may be blurred, a diary largely deals with externals and is used to passively record events; whereas a journal is about your inner-being, and is used as a tool for self-improvement.

One of the major benefits of keeping a journal is that it lets you monitor your own internal processes, helping you to resolve any long-standing conflicts (or wrong beliefs) you have. It does this by helping you to see the changes taking place in your life, *changes that will only become evident through rigorous self-examination.*

And more important, a journal can help you to understand your dreams and gain valuable insight from them, putting you in touch with your higher self, which is responsible for creativity, wisdom, and for orchestrating the events in your life.

In short, keeping a journal turns your life from a seemingly random succession of events into a well-defined school. You begin to see the lessons in your life and put them into practice.

Exercise Number 3: Create a Journal

The first step is to physically get yourself a suitable journal. There are many paper-based and/or software-based journals available today. Just be sure to select one that can be divided into sections, as recommended below:

Section 1—Your daily log: Here, you make brief entries during the day, preferably immediately after an event has taken place. The key is to record any internal events that you feel are important. Include your emotions, reactions, inactions, thoughts, realizations, and interactions with technology, people, or situations, and the internal effects they had upon you. And, if there was an external trigger, record just enough of it to make sense of the entry.

Section 2—Your dream journal: Here you record any impressions, fragments, or complete dreams that you recall. Keep the journal by your bed and record anything that you remember. Dreams are one place where your intuitive, creative self seeks to establish communication with you. Thus, by making this effort, you begin to come into conscious communion with parts of yourself that transcend your normal conscious intelligence.

Section 3—Questions you need to answer: These can relate to any area of your life whatsoever—technology, work, relationships, spirituality, creativity, and so on. Actually, you are asking your higher-self for the answers.

Write your entry here in the form of a question. Date it and leave it. Then pay attention to your dreams, the events of the day, and your own internal insights and thought processes. The various parts of the journal fit beautifully together to give you the answers you seek.

Just *believe* that an answer will come. If nothing happens, simply repeat the process the next day with the same question! Be insistent. The answer will eventually appear.

Section 4—Your life cycles section: You review your life and try to describe it in terms of the big cycles that you have experienced. It may have been a technology cycle, relationship cycle, an employment/career cycle, or a cycle of religious affiliation. It differs for each person.

Think about your life and recognize the major cycles. For example, it may be your experiences with technology, fifteen-year marriage, your ten-year career with ABC Corp., etc. Within each major cycle, write the main events that made it up as a series of brief entries.

If you do this properly, you should also be able to identify minor cycles within the major. Do this also for the current cycle that you are living in right now.

Of course, many different cycles overlap each other in our lives. The point is simply to begin to get a perspective on the major movements within your life that have brought you to where you are today.

Just remember that you are trying to get from the *what is* to the *what will be* side of the great technological divide, and that you need to be to be aware of what is working and what is not.

So, being able to see the large cycles and subcycles helps you to achieve a much-expanded consciousness and context for your life. You see how the events of life seem orchestrated—as indeed they are —to lead you to learn many lessons and gain profound realizations.

You begin to realize where you failed to learn the lesson, and therefore, had to experience it all over again in another time and place until it finally sank in. In short, you gain perspective. In doing so, you become more empowered to lay out a grander vision for your future.

Section 5—Other: Add other sections as needed.

Think of your journal as a personal tool for self-growth and let it evolve as your needs and aspirations change. However, the important thing is just to get started and experience the benefits *now*.

Just remember that by taking just a few minutes a day to add to your journal can make you feel better because it will give you the benefit of doing something specifically for yourself.

Added note:

When using your journal, remember that it is *private*. Therefore, say what you wish, openly, and do not censor yourself. This is the one place where you can speak freely so encourage yourself to do so. At the same time, keep the journal in a safe place (or password protect it if you are using a software-based journal) so that others can't access it!

Notes Page

CHAPTER 6
Mind-Set Adjustment Number 4

The fourth mind-set adjustment is to share your plans with everyone you know.

Remember, *set the stage by making the intention and assuming the role.*

Tell everyone, including your closest friends, aunts, uncles, cousins, and anyone else who will listen to you about your plans. It is amazing how committed you can become especially when it comes to avoiding any embarrassment.

So make the *intention* and then *act* upon it by assuming the role and by living in the *present.*

Just remember that regret and shame come from dwelling in the *past*; whereas worry and anxiety come from living in the *future.* And that true peace of mind comes from living in the present. The more you become aware of the present, the more it becomes part of your daily routine.

Just be careful that you don't compare yourself to others because there will always be people who have more clients, make more money, and outshine you when it comes to the use of technology.

If you do, you will only end up feeling frustrated and constantly chasing success. Instead, make plans that feel natural to you and prepare yourself by learning how to embrace change.

Real Success Shows Up When Time Is Devoted to Becoming Great

To make the process easier, make an effort to become aware of your actions, dreams, fears, thoughts, and even your inactions by recording them in your journal. This will help you to deal with the things that you are not used to doing, such as telling everyone about your plans, learning and applying technologies, and helping others.

In fact, I have discovered that you really can't *change* something unless you know it exists. Just don't let your thoughts and fears get in your way! One way to do this is to review your journal in order to understand why you think the way you do, and in doing so, determine whether you are being influenced by outside forces or past events.

If you are, change your way of thinking, and be open to the fact that everything is possible. But whatever you do, find a way to separate yourself from any wrong thinking, because the things you believe might not hold any truth or value today.

Just remember that as humans we are born into this world without any preexisting knowledge about our universe, and in order to cope and survive, we must make observations and draw conclusions from them.

We need to make observations and generalizations, otherwise we wouldn't be able make sense of our surroundings. In other words, we create our own belief system, which becomes essential to our own survival, and perhaps even to our consciousness.

This does not mean that we should always trust what we believe. After all, our belief systems are based on our own subjective experiences, experiences that we convert into objective realities, which enable us to function.

Where

- **Subjective reality** is when we measure ourselves against the world and let others define us.
- **Objective reality** is when we see outside of our own belief system, without judging or measuring ourselves against others.

Once I understood this, I was able to function better by remaining objective about *life* and *technology* in general.

Obviously there is an infinite set of beliefs one can *believe* in, but the reality is that most would be nearly as useless as having no belief system at all. But as our belief systems grow in complexity, beyond simple common sense generalizations, these systems attempt to help us to explain and understand things.

That said, you still have to be careful how you interpret your feelings and experiences about technology as you forge ahead.

Try to see outside yourself. Try being objective, and don't take things personally or hold onto beliefs that only exist in your mind, which could prevent you from moving forward.

In other words, ignore your "internal self dialog" that promotes a subjective reality because it could be quite negative (or false).

Just be open to the fact that you will need to challenge your beliefs no matter how strongly you might feel about them. One way to do this is to develop a list of positive declarations that you can recite on a daily basis.

Here are a few that I recite:

- *I am* at peace with technology.

- *I am* richly blessed every day since my life purpose is aligned with my higher-self.
- *I am* the harmonious presence ever evading whatever situation I find myself in.
- *I am* open to constantly learning and improving my mental capacity.
- *I am* consciously aware that I have set in motion the full power and intelligence of my higher-self, producing the desired conditions that are thus self-sustained.

Whether you use these positive declarations or create a set of your own, it is important that you practice them. And if you do, I believe that you will be amazed at how effective they can be in terms of transforming your beliefs and attitude.

Just remember to make the intention, assume the role, and remain positive, and if you do, your journey should be a much shorter one. This is why it is so important to tell everyone about your plans; and to learn to deal with technological change.

A True Story

This reminds me of a time when I dreamt about conducting a seminar to a sold-out crowd at Toronto's largest indoor stadium. The next morning I made several telephone calls telling my family and my closest friends about my dream and how real it felt.

It was as though I had already conducted it, and I remember the energy and excitement I felt talking about technology to the thousands of people in attendance. The feeling was overwhelming and I couldn't let it go.

Three weeks went by, and then it happened. I received a telephone call from one of my major clients asking me to conduct a seminar at that exact location. Needless to say I was in shock! Although the actual seminar was to be held in the adjoining hotel, and thirty people were to attend, it didn't matter. I felt that this was okay, knowing that we are never given more that we can handle. And I knew that a crowd of thirty was just perfect for me at that time.

Needless to say, I was extremely grateful for the opportunity.

Since then, I have recorded many more such happenings in my journal, and I never forget to tell anyone who would listen about my plans.

Exercise Number 4: Make the Intention

An intention is to have in mind a purpose (or plan) to direct the mind to aim for something you want to manifest.

People who lack intention often stray without meaning or direction. But with it, all of your inner (or guiding) forces can align to make even the most impossible, possible.

As I stated before, my intention is to *help others to gain a competitive advantage through the innovative use of digital technologies and best practices.*

But to achieve (or manifest) something for yourself, you must transform the conversation—*in your mind*—about fear and uncertainty, into one of hope and possibility, followed by action and results.

The key is to know where you are so that you can design the appropriate strategy for getting to the place you want to be.

Although there are many unknowns, there has never been a more important time than *now* to live your dream. So, start by setting your intention!

Here are some examples:

- Before you get out of bed, you can intend to have a fun or productive day.
- Before you leave the house, you can intend to have a good day with technology.
- Before you start your car, you can intend to have a safe ride to work.
- Before you enter your workplace, you can intend to learn something new or be helpful to others.

Four intentional steps for creating your own intention:

1. Get clear about something you want and write it down.
2. Share your intention with someone in a way that will hold you accountable to taking action.
3. Do something today to demonstrate your commitment to your intention.
4. Acknowledge that you did what you said you would, and then, take the next step.

By setting an intention, you make it clear to yourself and others just what you plan to do. Set an intention to redefine what it means to be serious about your dreams.

Notes Page

CHAPTER 7

Mind-Set Adjustment Number 5

The fifth mind-set adjustment is to actively look for opportunities to apply what you have learned. Begin by asking friends, family, and business associates who they might know that could use your help.

Remember to *expand your comfort zone.*

Your comfort zone (what you feel comfortable doing) is always in a state that is either expanding or contracting.

At an early age, I learned to get out in the world and do what I felt uncomfortable doing; and when I did, I felt far less inhibited, which allowed me to live a much richer and fuller life.

In other words, getting out in the world helped me to spend more time expanding than contracting.

Don't be afraid to ask for what you want, even though you might feel uncomfortable at first. Ever hear the phrase, "The squeaky wheel gets the grease"?

It is the same reason that children ask their parents for the same thing over and over again, because they know Mom and Dad will eventually cave in.

The truth is that this concept works even for adults. So, if there is something in the world you want, ask for it, or at least ask *how* to get it.

Contrary to what you might believe, people are generally open to helping others especially, if they sense that that person is on a path of self-discovery and/or self-improvement.

However, finding opportunities takes a little detective work, and the approach you take will vary depending on whether you are working for someone else or are trying to prove yourself as an entrepreneur.

If you are working for someone else, you could try the following:

- Let your boss know that you have been sharpening your technology-related skills and that you are looking for some real-world experience to take it to the next level. It never hurts to advertise (or blow your own horn).
- Volunteer for an upcoming project. Ask your boss for permission to approach the project prime to see whether he or she would be willing to involve you in some way.
- Develop something (a spreadsheet, a mind-map, etc.) that will help you, your department, or company to be more efficient, more effective and more productive.
- Demonstrate what you have learned by helping others. People will notice and it won't be long before others begin to approach you looking for some help, or to work on a project.

If you are an entrepreneur, you could try the following:

- Find people who will refer jobs to you. If they send you nightmare jobs, make sure they're balanced out with rewarding (profitable) ones. Just be sure to express your gratitude for any and all referrals.
- Establish a consistent rate structure across all of your accounts. This will help you to avoid setting any unwanted precedents while helping you to maintain your integrity.

- Take some risks. It is amazing how much you can really do once you make a commitment, even though you might think that you are in over your head.

Exercise Number 5: Expand Your Comfort Zone

I could say, "Just do it!"

But I won't because doing so infers that you have to force yourself or be coerced into doing something you may not be ready to do. And instead of enhancing your skills and learning to hold yourself accountable, you would be met with more and more resistance.

Believers in the law of attraction know that what you focus on expands, and in terms of comfort zones, what you push against (or resist) gets stronger, not weaker. For a conscious creator, personal growth is about getting rid of your fear first by letting go of any uncertainty, self-judgment, self-doubt, and limiting beliefs before you look for ways to create your new reality.

The truth is that it's all about learning to feel good about *you*. For when you do, you will find it a lot easier to step outside your comfort zone, build your confidence, self-respect, and learn to take appropriate (or calculated) risks.

Just remember that when you feel good about yourself, you will be inspired to take action.

Here are a few things that you can try:

- **Change things up**—Most of us start each day with a strong cup of caffeinated coffee. For something different, try decaffeinated instead, or—gasp!—water. Sure, those first few days will be brutal. But after that, believe it or not, your body will adjust. If you don't already exercise in the morning, try walking ten thousand steps a day. You'll be surprised at how much energy it gives you for the rest of the day, and you might even be surprised by the amount of weight you could lose.

- **Make new friends**—It's easy to talk to the same people every day. It's tougher to open your mind up to different people. The solution is this: make a point of making new acquaintances. At work, this means a concerted effort to strike up conversations with people in other parts of the office. After hours, it might mean talking to people in coffee shops, joining new clubs, or becoming friendlier with other parents at your child's hockey games.

- **Try (or retry) something you swore you'd never do again**—Everyone tries new stuff and fails; only the truly brave (and babies) get up and try again. This process is the quintessential way of stepping out of your comfort zone. First, identify an activity you've sworn off. Maybe it's computing, learning a new software package, or eating healthy food.

Next, do what you must to give the activity a chance. Line up a lesson. Go with friends. All the while, remember that baby steps are better than no steps at all; often the biggest obstacle is the mere process of trying.

Notes Page

CHAPTER **8**

Mind-Set Adjustment Number 6

The sixth mind-set adjustment is to find a *challenge buddy*. A challenge buddy is someone who is willing to help test your theories, concepts, or abilities in a chosen area.

Remember, don't go it alone. Find a challenge buddy!

Before desktop computers arrived on the scene back in 1981, I decided to build a working replica of a popular computer from parts I purchased at an electronics parts depot.

At that time, I was serving on the board of directors of a condominium corporation where I met John. And, as it turned out, John was the proud owner of the same type of computer. It didn't take us very long to realize that we could leverage our knowledge of computers by sharing what little we knew with each other. And to accelerate the process, we joined a local computer club—a special interest group (or SIG)—and formed a few alliances with other computer enthusiasts. Soon after, we found ourselves teaching others and helping entrepreneurs by applying what we knew by solving business-related problems for a small profit.

This experience taught us a few lessons:

- Make a commitment to find a challenge buddy: There are people out there who are in the same place (or position) as you, and many of them are willing to help.

- Make a commitment to invest the requisite amount of time to learn something new and to practice by consciously applying it. And don't forget to share your newfound knowledge/skills with your challenge buddy.
- Make a commitment to stand up to the challenge, learn from your failures, and continue with your efforts. Remember, failure isn't an option!
- Make a commitment to simplify your life and accept the fact that you need to allow a controlled amount of complexity into it.

Just remember that Rome wasn't built in a day!

Exercise Number 6: Find a Challenge Buddy

If you have trouble motivating yourself to take action on a dream, goal, or task, I encourage you to find a challenge buddy.

Simply put, a challenge buddy is someone who is well aware of your goals and knows you fairly well, someone who will help you achieve your goals by sharing their knowledge and experiences with you.

So go out and find your challenge buddy today. Just remember that it should be someone who knows you pretty well and is aware of your goals, fears, desires, and dreams.

Together, you can make huge leaps in your personal growth!

Notes Page

CHAPTER 9

Mind-Set Adjustment Number 7

The seventh mind-set adjustment is to be grateful.

Remember, be grateful for everything and everyone that comes into your life.

Sir Isaac Newton once said that "every action always has an opposite or equal reaction." When I first heard this, I didn't realize how significant it was or how I could actually use it to enhance my own life and the lives of others.

That is until I started to study the law of attraction only to find that I was using Sir Isaac Newton's fundamental law of motion without even realizing it.

In fact it wasn't until I discovered the link between the law of attraction and *gratitude* that I discovered that he was speaking the absolute truth.

The truth being that when a person gives thanks, it causes an opposite reaction of receiving. And what you receive is equal to the amount of gratitude you've given.

This discovery helped me to understand what the authors of books I've read meant when they spoke about the law of attraction; and that gratitude was the key for making it work.

If you are not familiar with the law of attraction, it is a powerful mental tool that works by having you focus on something that you want while visualizing that you already have it.

The process itself helps to increase your awareness for recognizing opportunities that occur around you. These opportunities will then assist you in bringing what you want (or attracting) them into your physical reality.

However, this will only work if you are appreciative enough to allow gratitude to be expressed.

For example, you can start by being grateful for

- All the things you already have
- All the people that came into and out of your life
- All the resources (including the technology) you have access to
- All the dreams and desires you have
- And whatever else, you'd like to add

The real secret is to use the words "thank you," to express your gratitude. But, when I say that, I do not mean that you should just mouth the words.

But instead, express your gratitude with feeling and true sincerity.

Although I feel that I should tell you more about the law of attraction and how to become a more grateful and loving person, my presence (or inner-self) tells me that I need to leave this up to you and you alone.

I say this knowing that whatever you need will be released to you when your presence feels that you are ready to receive and/or can handle it.

This could be in the form of a lesson to be learned, success with technology, an innovative idea, some unexpected income, a timely meeting, or something else that you either need or want.

Just learn to be patient and when something does manifest itself, remember to express your gratitude with feeling!

A True Story

This reminds me of a story that I often tell about purchasing good reference books to help with my business. Although some of my purchases are based on a need or a referral from a friend, others are based on an instinct or feeling that comes over me.

The interesting thing is that this feeling comes as I scan the book titles on the shelves. It's as if the books in question give off some kind of energy (magnetic energy) that attracts me to them.

I like to believe that this energy emanates from the authors and that it is my presence that drew my attention to them; otherwise, I would have probably passed over them because I couldn't see the value in purchasing them at the time.

What I discovered, though, was that many of these books ended up being the best choices for me. I just didn't know it at the time. But they were filled with information and/or tips that I used to gain a competitive advantage in my field, and that I used to help others through the use of best practices.

Needless to say, I expressed my gratitude to the authors for publishing their books; and to my presence (inner-self) for drawing my attention to them. I am eternally grateful!

Please note that I decided to share this story with you to increase your awareness of them and to help you to understand how important it is to get in touch with, and to trust, the feelings that you have.

Just remember to express your gratitude (with feeling) and tune-in to your presence (inner voice) that is always at work.

Notes Page

Exercise Number 7: Express Your Gratitude

When I was fifteen-years old, my mother told me that being consciously grateful is essential to a happy life. She told me that being grateful would help me to be a more positive and optimistic person. And if I changed from being selfish (which I was) to being grateful, I would attract more positive people, events, and opportunities into my life. That would be my reward.

Of course, I followed her advice. After all, she is my mother!

But it wasn't until I met Carol (my wife) that I fully understood what being grateful meant on a spiritual level. And when I interpreted what she told me, I came to the following realization: by being grateful, I was tipping my hat to my presence (the universe for some), who in turn would be like, "Wow, this guy really appreciates the goodness in his life, so I am going to send him some more goodness!"

The point is, I truly believe this. I truly believe that being grateful opens you to more opportunities to be grateful for. This has proven true in my personal life, and these are the steps I took to get into the mind-set I am in today. Please feel free to repeat them!

Be Thankful

Look around you. No matter who you are, there is something that you can be thankful for: a roof over your head, the technology you use, the car you drive, the clothes you wear, the food you eat, your family and friends, your health. Each of these things are truly a gift.

When you begin to recognize the goodness in your life and make a conscious effort to be grateful for those things, you will see that every day there is more and more to be thankful for.

If you honestly think there is nothing to be thankful for in your life, you're not trying hard enough. At the very least, you should be thankful you are fortunate enough to be reading this.

Turn Negatives into Positives

Being grateful makes it really easy to turn negatives into positives. This is a great practice to get into, and that's what it is, a practice. Many of us aren't taught to be actively grateful, so you have to make an effort. Next time you feel like complaining about your job, be grateful you have one. When you are ticked off because your mom is coming down hard on you about your grades, but be grateful you have a parent who cares. Your attitude and your worldview is shaped by how you think. If you can change the way you think, you can change your world.

Appreciate Challenges

A person is not defined by what happens to them in their life. A person is defined by how they deal with what happens in their life. We all have hardships to overcome, and with each hardship, you have a choice. You can either choose to let it break you or choose to let it make you. I'm not saying not to grieve when bad things happen or that you have to be happy all the time, but what I am saying is that you have to use the challenges in your life to make yourself a better person. With every moment of suffering you endure, there is something to learn. We must be grateful for those opportunities, because that is how you grow and become a stronger person.

Love Everyone

Don't confuse this with having to like everyone. There is no way you're going to like everyone, just like there is no way everyone is going to like you. But you can love every person that comes into your life because each of them can teach you something about yourself and the world. Be aware of yourself, your relationships, and how they make you feel. The people who bother you most usually have the most to teach you. Love your scatterbrained lab partner because he is teaching you to be more patient. Love the rude girl at the party because you know her evil glares stem from her own insecurity. Love your jerky coworker because they are giving you the opportunity to practice standing up for yourself and voicing your opinions.

Treasure Moments—No Matter How Big or Small

I just chased my dog all over the house, and after he got tired, he rolled over on his back with the biggest smile on his tiny face. It's these simple things, like making my loved one's life more enjoyable, that make my life more enjoyable. Relish in the moments you spend with friends, laughing at a dinner party. Thank God for your parents' craziness during the holidays because it is in part what has made you what you are, for spending time outside because you love the sunshine. For each moment you take the time to be present in will help you garner a deeper appreciation for life.

Ideas for Daily Exercises in Gratitude

Sometimes just telling yourself to think a new way can be hard, so here is an idea to help make thinking gratefully easier: Add a gratitude-section to your journal. Every night, write down ten things you are thankful for that day and how they affect your life. Even if it's just the budding tulips outside your window, that's something to be thankful for. They are giving you a prettier view, aren't they?

Notes Page

Chapter 10

What's In It for Me?

We are all only one adjustment away from making our lives work. And, in order to make that adjustment you need to find the purpose (or real reason) for wanting to succeed.

As I indicated earlier, when you take action, there is an undeniable connection between what you do and what you get. In other words, actions determine outcomes; outcomes determine your level of success.

But in order to achieve this, you must take complete ownership and operate with purpose.

Purpose is what will inspire and motivate you.

- It will help you to persevere through problems and/or setbacks and keep pushing you forward.
- It will help you to break through the ceiling of achievement.
- It will help you to take ownership of your outcomes by forcing you to hold yourself accountable.

Purpose Will Help to Define You!

Just remember that "accountable" people achieve results that others can only dream about. And when life happens, and it will, you can be either the author (or creator) of your life or the victim of it.

In times of change, "What's in it for me?" is the question you need to answer. In fact, great leaders talk about change as a movement, a movement toward a future that promises not just something different but hopefully, something better.

Just remember that change isn't what really troubles most people. It's the transition from the present to the future that does. Think of it as a psychological rite of passage during which people come to terms with the new situation (the change).

This is what I was referring to when I came up with the seven mind-set adjustments and talked about moving from the *what is* (the present) to the *what will be* (the future) side of the great technological divide.

Now that you know that every change begins with an ending, it is time for you to step up to the challenge to validate that journey. Your journey!

And to find your true purpose simply answer the all-important question: "What's in it for me?"

Exercise Number 8: Finding Your Purpose

Please answer this final question.

1. What's in it for me?

Notes Page

Chapter 11

The Final Word

You will know when you have arrived when you feel a sense of freedom and of authenticity come over you; and when you feel empowered instead of being controlled by others or by the technology you use.

It stands to reason that if you focus on something that you love and are good at, you are much more likely to feel like you can conquer and/or achieve anything.

And as you move away from the *what is* to the *what will be* side of the great technological divide, any fear or uncertainty you had will start to fade away.

Just remember that *you* make yourself feel the way you feel. So feel good about yourself and about the technology you use. After all, you do have power to change your reality and create a better life for yourself and for your loved ones.

I hope that this book inspires you to act and to make a commitment to yourself so that you can be who you are truly meant to be.

Wishing you all the best!

Regards,

Nick Kenyeres, Dipl.T., BAS
Digital lifestyle coach and author

About the Author

Nick Kenyeres is an entrepreneur, adjunct professor, technology coach, and author.

Operating as a digital lifestyle coach, Nick steadfastly believes in helping individuals and companies gain a competitive advantage through the innovative use of digital technologies and best practices.

His intentions are to improve the way we think, live, and experience life in a world of technological expansion. He believes in breaking through the current constraints in our thinking that hold us back from realizing all that we desire.

Death, taxes, and now technology are our inevitable certainties. Nick's seven mind-set adjustments show us a simple way to shift into the realization of our dreams and our ability to embrace the positive application of technology in today's world for success as we define it.

Nick dedicates his time to his writing and to helping others make peace with technology. His writings comfort and guide us to expand our thinking beyond fear, allowing us to embrace the positives this certainty affords us.

He currently holds a three-year electronics engineering technology diploma, a business administration certificate, and a four-year bachelor of applied science degree in technology management.

Nick has worked in both the telecommunication and training industries, and continues to serve others as an adjunct professor and digital lifestyle coach.

Always remember: *Fool yourself into changing your beliefs or way of thinking until you reach a point where you see incremental improvements and become motivated by that.*